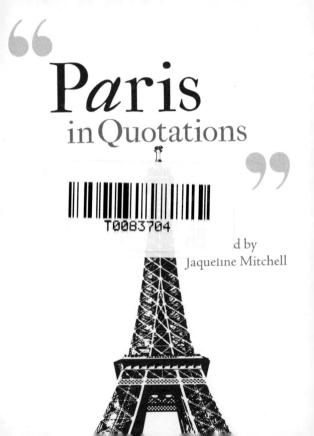

Paris
in Quotations

d by
Jaqueline Mitchell

First published in 2016 by the
Bodleian Library
Broad Street
Oxford OX1 3BG
www.bodleianshop.co.uk

ISBN: 978 1 85124 410 2

Selection and arrangement © Bodleian Library
Cover design by Dot Little
Designed and typeset by Rod Teasdale in 11 on 13pt Jenson
Printed and bound by L.E.G.O. spa, Vicenza

British Library Catalogue in Publishing Data
A CIP record of this publication is available from
the British Library

… all roads lead to Paris.

Gertrude Stein
(1874–1946)

66

After you've lived in Paris for a while, you don't want to live anywhere, including Paris.

John Ashbery
(b. 1927)

At last I have come into dreamland.

Harriet Beecher Stowe
(1811–1896)

66

But the brilliant parts of Paris, of which Frenchmen are in the habit of boasting, attract our attention only to divert it from the narrow, crooked lanes, and the filth of the other parts of the town. Paris sports a clean shirt-front merely to hide the uncleanliness of its general nature.

Max Schlesinger
(1822–1881)

66

Could anyone conceive such a
creation, such a land of continuous
gaiety? It is a masterpiece among
cities, the last word in pleasure.

Charlie Chaplin
(1889–1977)

66

Good Americans, when they die,
go to Paris.

Attributed to
Thomas Gold Appleton
(1812–1884)

We shall travel many thousands of miles after we leave here, and visit many great cities, but we shall find none so enchanting as this.

Mark Twain
(1835–1910)

The best of America drifts to Paris. The American in Paris is the best American.

F. Scott Fitzgerald
(1896–1940)

… ten years of Paris would improve an orang-outang.

Edward Bulwer-Lytton
(1803–1873)

The opulence of the French capital
arises from the defects of its
government and Religion.

Edward Gibbon
(1737–1794)

Paris adores money, but hates the monied… Revolutionary she may be in opinion, but in matters of habit and behaviour there is no city more conservative.

Paul Morand
(1888–1976)

" In Paris, if one has money, one has everything. Paris – it is not London, where to succeed one must be truly successful. "

Arnold Bennett
(1867–1931)

Paris is a city of gaieties and pleasures, where four fifths of the inhabitants die of grief.

Nicolas Chamfort
(1741–1794)

London is a riddle. Paris is an explanation.

G.K. Chesterton
(1874–1936)

Parisians have so many interests that,
in the end, they have none.

Honoré de Balzac
(1799–1850)

"

From what I have seen of the Parisians,
I am convinced that they require, if not
a despot, at least an absolute monarch
to reign over them.

Maria Edgeworth
(1768–1849)

When Paris sneezes, Europe catches cold.

Prince Metternich
(1773–1859)

Behold me on the vaunted scene of Europe!

Thomas Jefferson
(1743–1826)

Paris is a beast of a city to be in – to those who cannot get out of it.

William Hazlitt
(1778–1830)

66

In Paris everyone wants to be an actor;
no one is content to be a spectator.

Jean Cocteau
(1889–1963)

"

Fashion is more tyrannical at Paris
than at any other place in the world...
You must observe, and conform to all
the *minutiae* of it, if you will be in
fashion there yourself; and if you are
not in fashion, you are nobody.

Philip Dormer Stanhope,
4th Earl of Chesterfield
(1694–1773)

The head monkey at Paris puts on a traveller's cap, and all the monkeys in America do the same.

Henry David Thoreau
(1817–1862)

… this is no world for you unless you have your pockets lined and your delicacies perverted.

Henry James
(1843–1916)

In Paris, our lives are one masked ball.

Gaston Leroux
(1868–1927)

It is the most extraordinary place in the world!... I cannot conceive any place so perfectly and wonderfully expressive of its own character; its secret character no less than that which is on its surface.

Charles Dickens
(1812–1870)

66

To breathe Paris is to preserve the soul.

Victor Hugo
(1802–1885)

Paris which is so imperfect, but which
is the only true town in the world.

Giacomo Casanova
(1725–1798)

I never rebel so much against France as not to regard Paris with a friendly eye; she has had my heart since my childhood... I love her tenderly, even to her warts and her spots.

Michel de Montaigne
(1533–1592)

The variety of Paris is matched by the energy, the voraciousness, and passion of its population.

Edmund White
(b. 1940)

66

This is my life in Paris ... An education
in style, glamour, gastronomy and grace
in a place where even the asparagus
spears are exquisite.

Janelle McCulloch

Paris is the middle-aged woman's paradise.

Arthur Wing Pinero
(1855–1934)

I can never look upon this city without strong emotion; it has been all my life to me... Paris has made me.

George Moore
(1852–1933)

Though I often looked for one, I finally had to admit that there could be no cure for Paris.

Paula McLain
(b. 1965)

Ennui is the enemy, and I confess that I cannot understand how anyone can feel bored in Paris. It seems to me that you have to work hard to concoct a share of boredom for yourself, because there's none to be had on the market.

Paris Guide
(1867)

As an artist, one has no other home in Europe than Paris.

Friedrich Nietzsche
(1844–1900)

The life of the young artist here is
the easiest, merriest, dirtiest
existence possible.

W.M. Thackeray
(1811–1863)

… of all capitals in the world, Paris must afford the most delightful residence to a mere literary lounger.

Sir Walter Scott
(1771–1832)

… cities are the very devil, Elizabeth,
if one is embalmed in them.

Katherine Mansfield
(1888–1923)

There is no city like Paris, no crowd like a Parisian crowd, to make you feel your solitude if you are alone in its midst!

George du Maurier
(1834–1896)

Back home you may be somebody but in Paris you are a nobody.

Honoré de Balzac
(1799–1850)

Paris is a vegetable patch. Where are my
wings, my airplanes, my ships, trains,
and the luminousness of New York?
I want to go away.

Anaïs Nin
(1903–1977)

Paris is the only city in the world where
starving to death is still considered an art.

Carlos Ruiz Zafón
(b. 1964)

... it is a pleasant place to live in when a
man wishes to dissipate.

George Romney
(1734–1802)

" … in that metropolis flourish a greater number of native and exotic swindlers than are to be found in any other European nursery.

W.M. Thackeray
(1811–1863)

Paris is a city where even the most outrageous story of incest and murder is greeted with a verbal shrug: *'Mais c'est normal!'*

Edmund White
(b. 1940)

Paris is Paris, there is but one Paris ... however hard living may be here and if it became worse and harder even – the French air clears up the brain and does one good – a world of good.

Vincent van Gogh
(1853–1890)

I am quite persuaded that there is no salvation for an honest soul beyond the gates of Paris.

Jean Molière
(1622–1673)

It's the only place in the world for a civilized man to live.

W. Somerset Maugham
(1874–1965)

America is my country and Paris is
my home town.

Gertrude Stein
(1874–1946)

"

Paris was the most human city we had.

Wyndham Lewis
(1882–1957)

Paris and *London*, in the first of which all wit is comprised in the power of ridiculing one's neighbours, and in the other every artifice is put in practice to escape it.

Hester Lynch Piozzi
(1741–1821)

66

Mortals wander, Parisians stroll.

Victor Hugo
(1802–1885)

In no place in the world is it so easy,
I believe, to enter into conversation
with strangers as in Paris.

Frances Trollope
(1779–1863)

... to allow so pretty a woman to go out by herself in Paris was just as rash as to leave a case filled with jewels in the middle of the street.

Marcel Proust
(1871–1922)

Paris is a paradise for the man over forty,
but it is not much fun for children.

Paul Morand
(1888–1976)

It is chaos, a throng in which all seek
pleasure yet few can find it – or so it
appeared to me.

Voltaire
(1694–1778)

> If ever a whole Nation was Mad in the World, this is the Time; the Confluence of Strangers to Paris is incredible, and the Accounts give of it are such as Posterity will take for mere Fable.

Daniel Defoe
(1660–1731)

Napoleon wanted to turn Paris into
Rome under the Caesars, only with
louder music and more marble.

Tom Wolfe
(b. 1931)

> [In New York] everyone conceals his secret life, whereas in Paris it was the exciting substance of our talks, intimate revelations and sharing of experience.

Anaïs Nin
(1903–1977)

Paris never changes: that is one of her
most precious secrets.

E.V. Lucas
(1868–1938)

Paris is a city of centralisation.

Bram Stoker
(1847–1912)

An eternal city, Paris! More eternal than Rome, more splendorous than Nineveh. The very navel of the world.

Henry Miller
(1891–1980)

Paris is a hard place to leave, even when
it rains incessantly and one coughs
continually from the dampness.

Willa Cather
(1873–1947)

Paris, city crowned above all others,
A fount, a well of sense and knowledge …
In truth, she is without peer.

Eustache Deschamps
(*c.*1340–1406)

But the best tongues are in Paris.

François Villon
(1431–1463)

Paris was a museum displaying
exactly itself.

Jeffrey Eugenides
(b. 1960)

Secrets travel fast in Paris.

Napoleon Bonaparte
(1769–1821)

66

Paris is so charming that I think of becoming a French poet!

Oscar Wilde
(1854–1900)

Paris is a mighty schoolmaster, a grand enlightener of the provincial intellect.

Mary Elizabeth Braddon
(1835–1915)

'*Fluctuat nec mergitur*': She is tossed by the waves, but does not sink.

Motto from the coat of arms of the City of Paris

The streets of Paris are not very good for the health.

Émile Zola
(1840–1902)

[In Paris] all people's thoughts seem to be on present diversion.

Lady Mary Wortley Montagu
(1689–1762)

There is an atmosphere of spiritual
effort here. No other city is quite like it.

James Joyce
(1882–1941)

66

Paris is, without doubt, one of the most charming and luxurious capitals in the world. It would be difficult to say whether Pleasure built Paris, or took up her abode within its walls after it was built.

Bradshaw's illustrated guide through Paris and its environs (1855)

I am savage enough to prefer the woods, the wilds, and the independence of Monticello, to all the brilliant pleasures of this gay capital [Paris].

Thomas Jefferson
(1743–1826)

66

I have never ceased to love it
[Montmartre]... It is a place where
you were always standing and
sometimes waiting, not for anything
to happen, but just standing.

Gertrude Stein
(1874–1946)

[Paris is] the biggest temple ever built to material joys and the lust of the eyes.

Henry James
(1843–1916)

"

Paris makes more than the law, it makes
the fashion; Paris sets more than the
fashion, it sets the routine... its books,
its theatre, its art, its science, its
literature, its philosophy, are the
manuals of the human race.

Victor Hugo
(1802–1885)

The most prominent feature in the character of a Parisian, is a peculiar *politesse*, which rarely fails to please, though it frequently borders on grimace.

The Stranger's guide to the French metropolis
(1816)

66

One of the saddest towns: weary of its now-mechanical sensuality, weary of the tension of money, money, money, weary even of resentment and conceit, just weary to death, and still not sufficiently Americanized or Londonized to hide the weariness under a mechanical jig-jig-jig!

D.H. Lawrence
(1885–1930)

… in Paris remember, when once in
society, you are always there.

Joseph Sheridan Le Fanu
(1814–1873)

66

It is better to starve in Paris than grow fat in Holland.

Leonard Merrick
(1864–1939)

A man who comes to Paris without directing his mind to dinners, is like a fellow who travels to Athens without caring to inspect ruins.

W.M. Thackeray
(1811–1863)

There is no place in the world like Paris. You must not think that I exaggerate when I speak in this way of the music here...

Wolfgang Amadeus Mozart
(1756–1791)

None will ever be a true Parisian who has not learnt to wear a mask of gaiety over his sorrows and one of sadness, boredom, or indifference over his inward joy.

Gaston Leroux
(1868–1927)

Their kindness and accommodation to strangers is unparalleled, and the hospitality of Paris is beyond anything I had conceived to be practicable in a large city.

Thomas Jefferson
(1743–1826)

Everybody comes back to Paris. Always.

Jean Rhys
(1890–1979)

Credits

The publisher gratefully thanks the many copyright holders below who have generously granted permission for the use of the quotations in this book. Every effort has been made to credit copyright holders of the quotations used in this book. We apologize for any unintentional omissions or errors and will insert the appropriate acknowledgement to any companies or individuals in the subsequent editions of the book.

p.1, Gertrude Stein, *The Autobiography of Alice B. Toklas* (1933), reprinted with the permission of Penguin Books (UK), Harcourt Brace & Co (USA); p.2, John Ashbery, *Selected Prose* (2004 ed.), reprinted with the kind permission of the author; p.3, Harriet Beecher Stowe, *Sunny Memories of Foreign Lands* (1854); p.4, Max Schlesinger, *Saunterings in and about London* (1853); p.5, Charlie Chaplin, *My Wonderful Visit* (1922), reprinted with the permission of the Chaplin Office; p.6, attr. to Thomas Gold Appleton; p.7, Mark Twain, *The Innocents Abroad* (1870); p.8, F. Scott Fitzgerald, from *Conversations with F. Scott Fitzgerald* (1927); p.9, Edward Bulwer-Lytton, *The Parisians* (1872); p.10, Edward Gibbon, *Memoirs of my Life* (1796); p.11, Paul Morand, *Paris to the Life* (1933), reprinted with the permission of Oxford University Press; p.12, Arnold Bennett, *The Lion's Share* (1916); p.13, Nicolas Chamfort, quoted in *The Cynic's Breviary: Maxims and Considerations from Nicolas De Chamfort*, ed. William G. Hutchison (1902); p.14, G.K. Chesterton, 'An Essay on Two Cities'. in *All Things Considered* (1908); p.15, Honoré De Balzac, 'The Girl with the Golden Eyes'; p.16, Maria Edgeworth, in a letter to Mrs Ruxton, July 1820; p.17, Prince Metternich, letter dated 26 January 1830; p.18, Thomas Jefferson, on arriving in Paris, 1784; p.19, William Hazlitt, *Notes of a Journey through France and Italy* (1826); p.20, Jean Cocteau, 'Le coq et l'arlequin' © 1918, 1979, 2009, Editions Stock; p.21, Philip Stanhope, *Letters to his Son*, 1737-68; p.22, Henry David Thoreau, *Walden, or Life in the Woods* (1906); p.23, Henry James, *Madame de Mauves* (1908); p.24, Gaston Leroux, *The Phantom of the Opera* (1909); p.25, Charles

Dickens, letter to Count D'Orsay, 7 August 1844. © Estate of Charles Dickens, reprinted with the kind permission of Commander Mark Dickens; p.26, Victor Hugo, *Les Miserables* (1862); p.27, Giacomo Casanova, *Memoirs* (1798); p.28, Michel de Montaigne, 'Of Vanity' (*c.*1580); p.29, Edmund White, *The Flâneur* © Edmund White 2001. Reproduced by permission of the author c/o Rogers, Coleridge & White Ltd., 20 Powis Mews, London W11 1JN; p.30, Janelle McCulloch, *La Vie Parisienne*, with permission of the author; p.31, Arthur Wing Pinero, *The Princess and the Butterfly* (1898); p.32, George Moore, *Memoirs of My Dead Life* (1906); p.33, Paula McLain, *The Paris Wife* (2010), printed with the permission of Little, Brown Book Group; p.35, Friedrich Nietzsche, 'Why I am So Clever', *Ecco Homo* (1908); p.36, W.M. Thackeray, quoted in *The Paris Sketch Book* (1831); p.37, Walter Scott, *Paul's Letters to his Kinsfolk* (1816); p.38, Katherine Mansfield, letter to the Countess Russell, 24 March 1922, reprinted with the permission of The Society of Authors, literary representative of the Estate of Katherine Mansfield; p.39, George du Maurier, *The Martian* (1897); p.40, Honoré De Balzac, *A Distinguished Provincial at Paris* (1901); p.41, Anaïs Nin, *Fire: from A Journal of Love: The Unexpurgated Diary of Anaïs Nin* (1996), UK and Commonwealth volume rights used by permission of Peter Owen Ltd, London. US rights, excerpts from FIRE by Anaïs Nin. Copyright © 1995, 1994, 1987 by Rupert Pole as Treasurer under the Last Will and Testament of Anaïs Nin; copyright © 1996 by Gunther Stuhlmann, copyright c 1996 by Rupert Pole by permission of Houghton Mifflin Harcourt Publishing Company. All rights reserved; p.42, Carlos Ruiz Zafón, *The Shadow of the Wind* (© 2004), reprinted with the permission of the author and The Orion Publishing Group; p.43, George Romney, letter to his son (1790); p. 44, W.M. Thackeray, quoted in *The Paris Sketch Book* (1831); p.45, Edmund White, *The Flâneur* © Edmund White 2001. Reproduced by permission of the author c/o Rogers, Coleridge & White Ltd., 20 Powis Mews, London W11 1JN; p.46, Vincent van Gogh, letter of 1886; p.47, Jean Molière, *Les Précieuses Ridicules* (1659); p.48, W. Somerset Maugham, *The Razor's Edge* (2000), reprinted with the permission of United Agents on behalf of The Royal Literary Fund (Maugham); p.49, Gertrude Stein, letter to Carl Van Vechten, 20 December, 1937, in *The Letters of Gertrude Stein and Carl Van Vechten 1913-1946*. © The Estate of Gertrude Stein, 1986, reprinted with the permission of Columbia University Press; p.50, Wyndham Lewis, *Tarr* (1931), reprinted with the permission of Bridgeman Art; p. 51, Hester Lynch Piozzi,

Observations and Reflections Made in the Course of a Journey through France, Italy, and Germany (1789); p.52, Victor Hugo, *Les Misérables* (1862); p.53, Frances Trollope, *Paris and the Parisians* (1836); p.54, Marcel Proust, *Swann's Way* (1913), translation by Scott-Moncrieff (1922); p.55, Paul Morand, *Paris to the Life* (1933), reprinted with the permission of Oxford University Press; p.56, Voltaire, *Candide* (1759); p.57, Daniel Defoe, from *Life and Recently Discovered Writings* (1869); p.58, Excerpt from 'Prologue' from *Bauhaus To Our House* by Tom Wolfe. Copyright © 1981 by Tom Wolfe. Reprinted by permission of Farrar, Straus & Giroux, Inc.; p.59, excerpt from *The Diary of Anais Nin*, Volume Three: 1939–1944. Copyright © 1969 by Anais Nin and renewed Rupert Pole and Gunther Stuhlmann. Reprinted by permission of Houghton Mifflin Harcourt Publishing Company. All rights reserved; p.60, E.V. Lucas, *A Wanderer in Paris* (1922); p.61, Bram Stoker, *The Burial of the Rats* (1896); p.62, Henry Miller, *Tropic of Cancer*, reproduced with permission of Curtis Brown Group Ltd, London on behalf of The Estate of Henry Miller. Copyright © Henry Miller 1934; p.63, from *Willa Cather in Europe* by Alfred A. Knopf (1956), reprinted with the permission of the Willa Cather Literary Trust; p.64, Eustache Deschamps, 'Ballade de Paris'; p.65, François Villon, 'Ballade of the Women of Paris'; p.66, Jeffrey Eugenides, *The Marriage Plot*, reprinted by permission of HarperCollins Publishers Ltd © 2011 Jeffrey Eugenides; p.68, Oscar Wilde, letter to W.H. Grenfell; p.69, Mary Elizabeth Braddon, *The Cloven Foot* (1880); p.71, Émile Zola, *Savage Paris* (1873); p.72, Mary Wortley Montagu, letter to Lady R., 10 October 1718; p.73, James Joyce, letter to Frank Budgen (1920); p.75, Thomas Jefferson, letter to Baron Geismer dated 6 September 1785; p.76, Gertrude Stein, *The Autobiography of Alice B. Toklas* (1933), reprinted with the permission of Penguin Books (UK), Harcourt Brace & Co (USA); p.77, Henry James, letter to Edward Warren dated 25 February 1898; p.78, Victor Hugo, *Les Misérables* (1862); p.80, D.H. Lawrence, *Lady Chatterley's Lover* (1928), reprinted by permission of Pollinger Limited (www.pollingerltd.com); p.81, Joseph Sheridan Le Fanu, *The Room in the Dragon Volant* (1872); p.82, Leonard Merrick, *A Chair on the Boulevard* (1919); p.83, W.M. Thackeray, 'On Some Dinners At Paris', for *Punch* (1849); p.84, W.A. Mozart, letter dated 1 May 1778; p.85, Gaston Leroux, *The Phantom of the Opera* (1909); p.86, Thomas Jefferson, *Autobiography* (1821); p.87, Jean Rhys, *Good Morning Midnight* (1939), reprinted with the kind permission of Ellen Ruth Moerman, and the Jean Rhys archive.